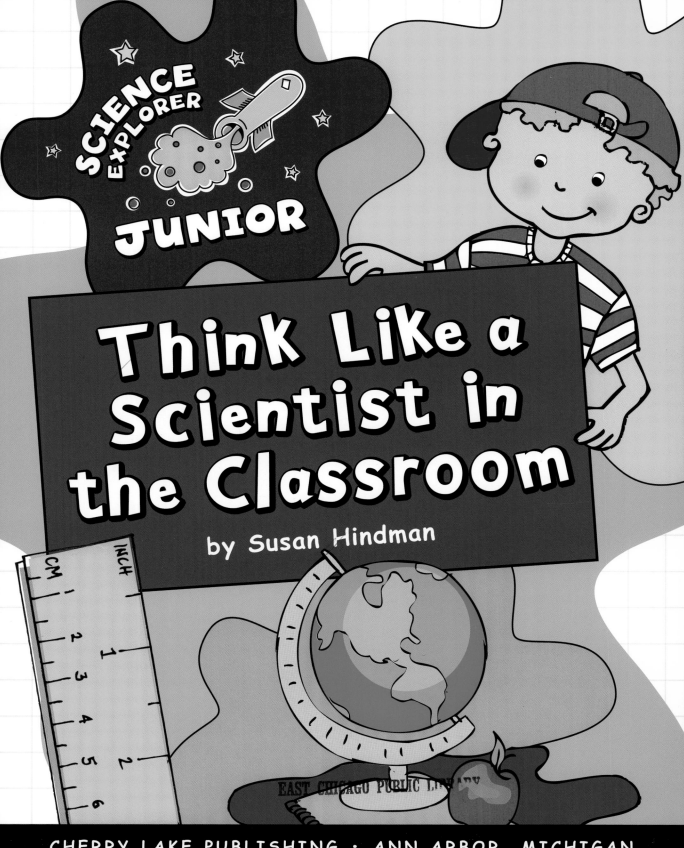

SCIENCE EXPLORER JUNIOR

Think Like a Scientist in the Classroom

by Susan Hindman

CHERRY LAKE PUBLISHING · ANN ARBOR, MICHIGAN

Published in the United States of America by Cherry Lake Publishing
Ann Arbor, Michigan
www.cherrylakepublishing.com

Content Editor: Robert Wolffe, EdD, Professor of Teacher Education,
Bradley University, Peoria, Illinois

Design and Illustration: The Design Lab

Photo Credits: Page 8, ©George Muresan/Shutterstock, Inc.; page 10,
©Suzanne Tucker/Shutterstock, Inc.; page 12, ©Andrey Armyagov/
Shutterstock, Inc.; page 13, ©Jozef Sedmak/Shutterstock, Inc.; page
16, ©Rob Marmion/Shutterstock, Inc.; page 18, ©NASA; page 23,
©naka Dharmasena/Shutterstock, Inc.; page 26, ©Ellen Isaacs/
Alamy; page 27, ©Darrin Henry/Shutterstock, Inc.; page 28, ©Benis
ArapovicShutterstock, Inc.

Library of Congress Cataloging-in-Publication Data
Hindman, Susan.
  Think like a scientist in the classroom/by Susan Hindman.
      p. cm.—(Science explorer junior)
  Includes bibliographical references and index.
  ISBN-13: 978-1-61080-170-6 (lib. bdg.)
  ISBN-10: 1-61080-170-9 (lib. bdg.)
  1. Science—Methodology—Juvenile literature. 2. Science—Experiments—
Juvenile literature. 3. Classroom Environment—Juvenile literature. I. Title.
II. Series.
  Q175.2.H56 2011
  507.8—dc22   2011003704

Cherry Lake Publishing would like to acknowledge the work
of The Partnership for 21st Century Skills. Please visit
www.21stcenturyskills.org for more information.

Printed in the United States of America
Corporate Graphics Inc.
July 2011
CLFA09

TABLE OF CONTENTS

Observe!

Vocabulary

Observe | Conclude | Experiment

Today is Wednesday.

AFRICA

What does your classroom look like?

Look around your classroom. Numbers, vocabulary words, and ideas are taped up on the walls. So are colorful pictures, maps, and posters. Maybe you see pictures of outer space, wild animals, and scenes from other countries.

Watch and listen to what's going on around you. Maybe you notice that half of the kids in your class are wearing blue shirts today. Maybe you hear that a fire truck driving by fast gets louder and then softer. You might hear someone's pencil land on the floor before the papers that fall with it. Maybe you realize that the sunlight coming through the window only shines on you at certain times of day. Does any of this make you curious to learn more? It's fun to dig deeper to find answers!

You can observe many things about your classmates.

STEP-BY-STEP

You can get your own answers by thinking like a scientist. Go step by step. You may have to repeat some steps as you go.

1. Observe what is going on.
2. Ask a question.
3. Guess the answer. This is called a **hypothesis**.
4. Design an **experiment** to test your idea.
5. Gather materials to test your idea.
6. Write down what happens.
7. Make a **conclusion**.

Don't forget your notepad.

Use words and numbers to write down what you've learned. It's okay if the experiment doesn't work. Try changing something, and then do the experiment again.

Write down everything you notice during the experiment.

The library is a great place to find information.

Scientists look for information before they start an experiment. They use this information as a place to start.

Where can you find information? A library is filled with books, magazines, and science videos.

You can find a lot of information in them. You can also talk to a librarian or a teacher. You can visit museums, too.

You can also find facts on the Internet. Be careful! Not everything on the Internet is the truth. Ask an adult to help you find the best places to look for information.

Parents, teachers, and librarians can help you use the Internet safely.

See It?

It can be easy to get distracted in your classroom.

To get your work done in class, you have to focus on your paper. But sometimes that's hard. There are a lot of distractions. And they're not always in front of you. You might be looking at your paper, but you can see things out of the corner of your eye. On your right, a boy leaned forward at his desk. On your left, a bright spot from a poster sneaks into view. How is all of this possible? Just how far to the side can you see when you look straight ahead?

Keep your eyes on your paper.

Your **peripheral vision** is at work when you see things that are not right in front of you. It's good at picking up motion. But it's not so good at picking up details like color and shape. Cells called cones catch light in the eye and help you see those details. The center of the eye is packed with cones. That's why color, shape, and motion appear clearly when you look straight at them. Cells

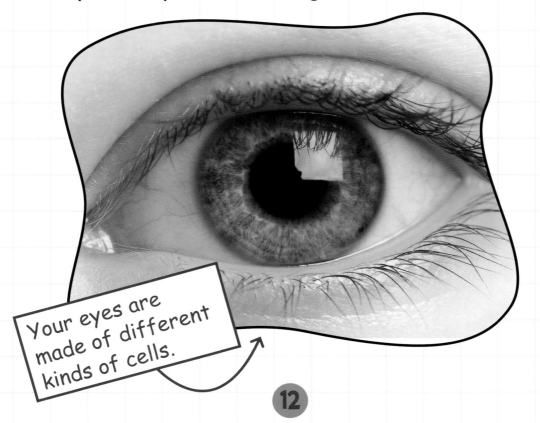

Your eyes are made of different kinds of cells.

called rods also help us see. They pick up black and white. There are more rods along the edges of your eye. That is why rods are very important to peripheral vision.

Famous painter Leonardo da Vinci studied vision. He wrote about how the eyes work together to gather information. He studied light, reflections, and shadows. He was the first person to notice that clear vision happens in only one place, called the line of sight. Peripheral vision is different than that. It is not clear vision. But you can still see things.

Leonardo da Vinci was born in 1452 and died in 1519.

Be sure to keep looking straight ahead.

Look straight ahead the entire time you do this. Hold your right arm out to the side and point your index finger up. You should not be able to see your finger. Now slowly move your right arm forward, keeping your finger pointed up. Keep looking straight ahead. Can you see your finger start to come into view? Write down your results. Try this experiment again when it is darker or lighter in the room. Compare your results. Can you think of other experiments you can do to learn more about your peripheral vision?

NOTES:
In the light:

In the dark:

Don't forget to record your results.

Got Energy?

The food you eat gives you energy for learning and playing.

Your body uses a lot of **energy** at school. But energy is used for more than just playing and thinking. Energy is what moves airplanes in the sky and trains over tracks. Energy plays songs on the radio and lights our homes. Energy comes in different forms, such as heat, light, and motion.

The Sun's energy is powerful. **Ultraviolet rays** are one form of energy that comes from the Sun. This light energy can break down the chemical bonds found in colors. When it does, it causes colors to fade. Do you think the Sun can make colored paper fade?

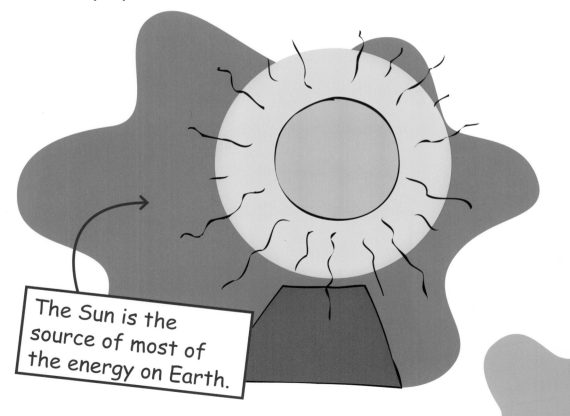

The Sun is the source of most of the energy on Earth.

The Sun gives off light that we can see and light that we can't see. We cannot see ultraviolet rays. Johann Wilhelm Ritter discovered them in 1801. How do you discover something that's invisible?

Ritter was doing experiments with silver chloride. This is a chemical that turns black when exposed to sunlight. He directed sunlight through a glass **prism** to create a **spectrum** of colors.

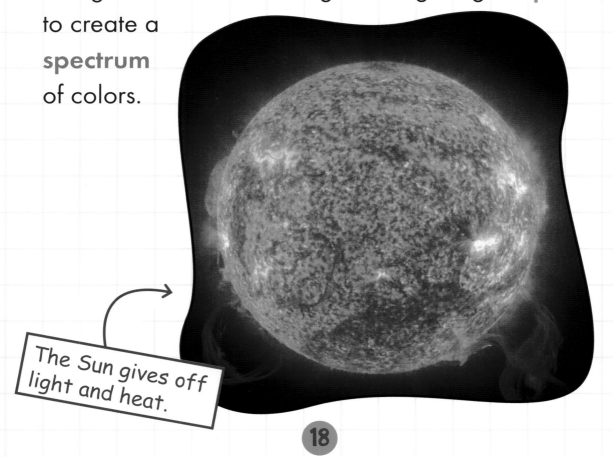

The Sun gives off light and heat.

He put the silver chloride in each color of the spectrum. The chemical didn't change color much in the red part of the spectrum. But it got darker in the violet part. Then he put it just outside the violet end of the spectrum. No sunlight was visible there. But the silver chloride turned black! This proved that invisible light existed outside the spectrum.

A prism shows all of the colors of visible light.

DO AN EXPERIMENT

You need two pairs of scissors and two sheets of construction paper for this experiment.

Lay two pieces of colored construction paper next to each other in a sunny place. Make sure they are the same color. Place a pair of scissors on top of each piece of paper. After two days, remove the scissors from one piece of paper. Look at the paper. Do you notice any difference in its color? In another two days, remove the scissors from the other piece of paper. Compare the two pieces of paper.

What did you see after you moved the scissors off the paper?

How Far?

Books sit flat on your desk. They won't slide off on their own. **Friction** determines how hard it is to make something start sliding. Friction is also the force that slows down two objects that are rubbed against each other. What happens if you push your books on a wood floor or on carpet? Do they go very far?

DO THE RESEARCH

Leonardo da Vinci wasn't just curious about vision. He also had questions about friction. He realized that friction was important to the way machines worked. He noticed a difference in the way materials moved. He made drawings of different parts of machines to show how friction played a role. He said that if something was smooth, it had less friction.

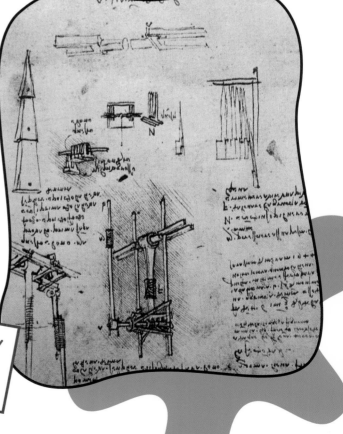

Da Vinci drew many different kinds of machines.

DO AN EXPERIMENT

Gather your materials before you begin experimenting.

Find a big book and a small book. Set them down on a floor that doesn't have carpet. Give the big book a push. See how far it goes. Leave it there, and then give the small book a push. Try to make sure you push as hard on the small book as you did on the big book. How far did it go? Measure the distances that the books traveled and write them down. Now find a floor with carpet and repeat the experiment. Compare the measurements. What did you learn? You probably saw that the small book traveled farther on both floor surfaces. The bigger, heavier book had more friction and didn't go as far.

Measure the distances carefully.

Your Big Idea!

Classrooms used to look very different from the way they look today.

In the late 1800s, students sat at desks that were **bolted** to the floor. Boys sat on one side of the room, and girls sat on the other. Desks were lined up in rows, one behind the other. Students faced the front of the room where the teacher stood. By 1930, desks could be moved around. In the 1960s, small, round tables were introduced into classrooms. That way, students could work together to learn. This was a very new idea!

Today students often work together in their classrooms.

Think about how your classroom is arranged.

You can think like a scientist to answer just about any kind of question. Look at the way the desks are arranged in your classroom. Do you see any problems? Is it hard for some students to get to the materials they need? Can everyone see the whiteboard? Observe and ask a question. Then make a hypothesis. See if you can come up with a better way to arrange the desks. Use a pencil and paper to draw different designs to test your idea.

Are you excited about finding an answer? That's the energy you need to think like a scientist!

Make a drawing of how you would arrange the desks in your classroom.

GLOSSARY

bolted (BOL-ted) fastened, attached

conclusion (kuhn-KLOO-zhuhn) the answer or result of an experiment

energy (EN-ur-gee) the ability to do work or to move an object

experiment (ik-SPER-uh-ment) a test of your idea

friction (FRIK-shun) the force that slows down moving things and turns the moving energy into heat energy

hypothesis (hye-PAH-thi-sis) a guess

peripheral vision (puh-RIF-uh-ruhl VIH-zhun) the area of vision that's outside the line of direct sight

prism (PRIH-zum) an object of glass, with ends that are triangles, that can break up light rays into colors of the rainbow

spectrum (SPEK-truhm) a series of colored bands formed when light is broken up after passing through a prism

ultraviolet rays (uhl-truh-VYE-o-let RAYZ) invisible rays of light

FOR MORE INFORMATION

BOOKS

Glass, Susan. *Analyze This! Understanding the Scientific Method*. Chicago: Heinemann Library, 2007.

Glass, Susan. *Prove It! The Scientific Method in Action*. Chicago: Heinemann Library, 2007.

Sadler, Wendy. *Energy: Get Moving!* Chicago: Raintree, 2006.

WEB SITES

Bill Nye The Science Guy
www.billnye.com
Find many experiments to do at home at the Web site of this popular television scientist.

Little Shop of Physics
littleshop.physics.colostate.edu/index.html
Check out the "Stuff to Try" experiments.

PBS: Evolving Classroom
www.pbs.org/kcet/publicschool/evolving_classroom/index.html
Learn what classrooms looked like 100 years ago.

INDEX

ABOUT THE AUTHOR

Susan Hindman has had a freelance editing and writing business in Colorado Springs, Colorado, since 1997. Before that, she worked for newspapers as a copyeditor, writer, and page designer. She has two grown daughters. Susan would like to thank Discovery Canyon Campus's elementary school and the scientists in her family for helping her think like a scientist.